# This Book Belongs To:

______________________________

www.ingramcontent.com/pod-product-compliance
Lightning Source LLC
Chambersburg PA
CBHW070736250726
48662CB00004B/1563